This Is My Song!

A
Collection
of
Gospel
Music
for
the Family

This Is My Song!

by Vy Higginsen
pictures by Brenda Joysmith

musical arrangements by Wesley Naylor

Crown Publishers, Inc., New York

To the next generation—long live the history and culture of our people!
—V. H.

In memory of my mother, Mrs. Ada Corine Smith
—B. J.

This book could not have been started—or completed—without the participation of the following: Wesley Naylor, Brenda Joysmith, Ken Wydro, Knoelle Higginson Wydro, Geraldine Higginson, Doris Troy, Joyce Davis, Randy Higginson, Kery Davis, Olga Dolly Wydro, Marie Brown, Desireé Coleman-Jackson, Charles Stewart, Richard Hartley, Reverend Dr. DeForest B. Soaries, Jr., Carolyn Nakano, Leonora Rush, Paul Vaughn, the *Mama* cast & staff, Wyatt Tee Walker, Deniece Williams, Shirley Caesar, Mavis Staples, Reverend Dr. Calvin O. Butts III, Dr. Portia K. Maultsby, Irene V. Jackson-Brown, Ph.D., Dr. Donald Byrd, Reverend Dr. William A. Jones, Sean Cort, the Crown/Random House family, Emile Charlap & Roger Blanc. *Thank you for your encouragement and support.*

Excerpts on pages 18, 40, 66, and 70 from *We'll Understand It Better By and By* by Bernice Johnson Reagon, (Washington, D.C., Smithsonian Institution Press, 1992). Reprinted by permission of the publisher.

Photographs on pages 9 (top), 10 (bottom), and 13 (bottom) courtesy of the Schomburg Collection; 9 (bottom) and 10 (top) courtesy of the Hogan Jazz Archive, Tulane University; 10 (center) and 11 (bottom) from the collection of Sherry Sherrod Du Pree; 11 (top), 12 (top), 13 (top), and 14 (top) from the collection of the New York Public Library for the Performing Arts at Lincoln Center; 12 (bottom), 14 (bottom), and 15 courtesy of Archive Photos.

Published by Crown Publishers, Inc., a Random House company,
201 East 50th Street, New York, New York 10022
CROWN is a trademark of Crown Publishers, Inc.
Manufactured in the United States of America

Hand-set music and music calligraphy by Christina T. Davidson

Library of Congress Cataloging-in-Publication Data
This is my song : a collection of gospel music for the family / [compiled and annotated] by Vy Higginsen ; illustrated by Brenda Joysmith.
1 score.
1. Sacred songs—Juvenile. 2. Gospel music. I. Higginsen, Vy. II. Joysmith, Brenda, ill.
M2193.G66   1995   93-34303

ISBN 0-517-59492-7 (trade)
        0-517-59493-5 (lib. bdg.)

10 9 8 7 6 5 4 3 2 1

First Edition

Contents

Introduction

My love for gospel music was nurtured and encouraged in church. My father was a Pentecostal minister in Harlem, and my memory takes me back to the songs that made me move, stand up, and clap my hands—so entranced that I wouldn't notice that they were red and swollen from clapping so hard and so long. Depending on the day, the time, and the church, there might be a piano, an organ, a drum, or only a tambourine—but the spirit, rhythm, words, and voices had a power that lifted my heart. That spirit will live with me forever.

Since that time in my father's church, gospel has moved from being sung only in churches and at church-related functions to being featured in Broadway shows, in concerts, and on radio and television. Many popular singers, from Dinah Washington to Aretha Franklin to Whitney Houston, began their careers singing gospel in church.

What is gospel? As a musical style, it has its roots in the spirituals of the nineteenth century. There is sometimes confusion about the difference between "spiritual" and "gospel" music. The "Negro folk spirituals," created in the 1800s by slaves, were sung from the heart and soul. They expressed love of God and belief in life after death, following the teachings of the Old and New Testament. The songs provided courage, inner strength, and hope for a better life in the future. Some of these spirituals were created on the spot—a kind of spontaneous combustion—while others were variations or adaptations— "arrangements," as it were—of African songs or white Protestant hymns.

Often, the singing would take the form of a call and response, in which the soloist would sing a phrase that was then repeated by the group. Each soloist was free to improvise: to twist, turn, inflect, and blend notes to express exactly what he or she was feeling at the moment. Accompaniment might be foot stomping and hand clapping or vocal sounds rather than actual instruments, so the human voice became the vehicle for communication. If you sang what you felt, the feeling could be even more important than the words, the text, or the original composition.

After the Civil War, these spontaneous creations were written down and arranged in an effort to preserve them. Performed as concert music, these formalized arrangements underwent aesthetic changes: syncopated and percussive rhythms, four-part harmony, and European vocal styling replaced the unison and improvised folk singing of slaves. Despite these changes, the essence of the folk spirituals remained, through the call-and-response structures and the original black dialect. Today these "arranged" sprituals continue to be performed throughout the world by black college choirs and professionals.

The gospel style puts the raw, spontaneous, immediate emotion back into this music—the hand clapping, the improvisation, the feeling. Gospel evolved during the Great Depression of the 1930s. Thomas A. Dorsey, a former blues and jazz pianist, became known as the "Father of Gospel." Dorsey was the first to combine the spirit of Negro folk spirituals with the rhythms and harmonies of blues and ragtime and the energy of urban life. This new body of sacred music he called "gospel."

Dorsey composed more than five hundred pieces, some of which have become gospel standards. No other gospel composer has as many published works in existence. Dorsey was able to capture the rhythm and sound of the African-American voice and shape the music to fit even the most average of singers.

Some gospel music can be hundreds of years old, the words very familiar, but what makes it gospel is its message and the way it is sung. The message is derived from the teachings of the New Testament, which emphasizes overcoming hardships through faith. In expressing this message, the gospel singer is allowed, and even encouraged, to improvise on the spot, to fill in the music with the emotion of the moment. Gospel is *how* you sing, play the piano, or move, inflect, or bend the note. Gospel is immediate, visceral, emotional—and this is what makes gospel alive and thrilling.

Because gospel music is so personal, so "in the moment," so unpredictable, it becomes a way of expressing emotion and deep beliefs. Gospel music is faith in action. When a singer allows the power of faith to come through, we call this "anointed."

Gospel is also the story of a culture in song. For black Americans, gospel music has much to do with being black, with the history and culture of a people oppressed for hundreds of years and still discriminated against today. With its roots in the songs that slaves working in the fields sang to liberate themselves from oppression, gospel goes back to the source of this oppression and fills the soul with emotion.

So for me, gospel is a matter of style and history—and, perhaps above all, feeling. As the creator and producer of the gospel musical *Mama, I Want to Sing*, I have been constantly amazed and surprised at how powerful and universal gospel music is. Audiences in places from Venice to Tokyo to Istanbul, as well as in all four corners of America, have laughed and cried, jumped and shouted at the passion of gospel.

This book, with authentic arrangements by Wesley Naylor, musical director of *Mama, I Want to Sing*, is a collection of some of the most moving gospel standards. It is intended to document and preserve, and to encourage the current generation to understand and participate in, the rich cultural heritage of gospel. I trust it will help present and promote the energy and spirit of gospel music, which I have witnessed touching so many thousands of people the world over.

In the spirit!

Vy Higginsen

A Gospel Photo Album

The Fisk Jubilee Singers, a choir of college students, were established at Fisk University in Nashville, Tennessee, in the 1860s and still exist today. They went on tour for the first time in 1871, singing the standard European repertoire together with arranged Negro spirituals to raise money for their university. These first efforts were unsuccessful because of the European compositions, so they changed exclusively to Negro spirituals and dropped their European repertoire. This new repertoire was so well received that it prompted almost every black college in the United States to organize a group, a quartet, or a choir. In addition, their work helped preserve spirituals in concert form. Seen here are the Fisk Jubilee Singers of 1957–1958.

Professor Thomas A. Dorsey, the "Father of Gospel," was born in Villa Rica, Georgia, in 1899. He composed his first gospel song, "If You See My Savior," in 1926. It was inspired by the death of his young son. During the Depression, Dorsey coined the term "gospel," which means "good news," for his music and he began putting together jazz-ragtime rhythms with blues harmonies and tonality and sacred verse to create songs that spoke to poor black Americans and (unlike the blues) were optimistic in outlook. A composer, pianist, and organizer and conductor of choirs, he teamed up with another gospel pioneer, Theodore Frye, to form the first gospel chorus at Pilgrim Baptist Church in Chicago. He is considered to have set the standard for all gospel music. Professor Dorsey sang well into his old age and died in 1993.

9

The Roberta Martin Singers

Sallie Martin, the "Mother of Gospel," was born in Pittfield, Georgia, in 1896. Her mother was a singer who traveled with the church. In 1916 Sallie joined the Fire Baptized Holiness Church. At Holiness churches (also called Pentecostal or Sanctified), sermons were made up mainly of passionate singing, dancing, and shouting in prayer, and this helped shape Sallie Martin into a confident and dedicated gospel singer with a rough, growly voice and an independent spirit. In the 1920s, she joined Professor Thomas Dorsey's group in Chicago, and she eventually toured with another group of singers. In 1932, she organized the Gospel Singers Convention along with Dorsey, and later began a music publishing house, as Dorsey did. She died in 1988 and is considered to have been a true pioneer of gospel music.

Roberta Martin was born Roberta Evelyn Winston in Helena, Arkansas, in 1907. She heard gospel music for the first time in 1933. Soon she became a pianist for the Young People's Choir at Ebenezer Baptist Church in Chicago and worked with Professor Thomas Dorsey and Theodore Frye. With help from these two men, and inspiration from Sallie Martin, Roberta organized the Martin-Frye Quartet, which later became the Roberta Martin Singers. Her group always included very talented musicians, and together with them, she introduced and developed a gospel choral sound that, unlike other groups at that time, included many female voices. Young musicians often joined the Roberta Martin Singers as a chance to "study" while coming through Chicago, and at different times her group included pianist James Cleveland and singer Dinah Washington. She also became a successful publisher of gospel music. Considered by some to be the greatest of all contributors to gospel music, she died in 1969.

Mahalia Jackson, born in 1911 in New Orleans, was known as the "Queen of Gospel." Her musical inspiration came from witnessing the worship at the Holiness church in New Orleans. At age sixteen, she began singing lead with the Greater Salem Baptist Church in Chicago, but soon quit to start a professional gospel group, the Johnson Singers, with her pastor's son. Jackson worked directly with Professor Thomas Dorsey. The singing style that she is known for—her slow hymns, bringing the blues sound to gospel—she learned from Dorsey while singing and demonstrating his songs. During her life, she gave gospel concerts all over the world, brought gospel to television, to radio, to Hollywood, and sold millions of records. Often asked by musicians to sing the blues, she never considered it once. "Blues are songs of despair," she was quoted as saying. "Gospel songs are the songs of hope." She died in 1972.

Sister Rosetta Tharpe was born Rosetta Nubin in Cotton Plant, Arkansas, in 1915. Raised in Chicago, she made her singing debut at age six as "Little Sister," singing with her mother. At that time, she could already play guitar. She would become known for her guitar playing and for her energy. Her musical style was more secular than that of many other gospel singers: she would play the blues on her guitar, or use a horn player's notes, or use the timing of a swing band. One of the first gospel singers to perform secular forms of music and with jazz bands, she played anywhere she could and recorded several records, but because of her involvement with secular music, she didn't find easy acceptance later when she tried to return to the church. She was considered a great inspiration by all gospel singers to come and was known for her famous grin. She died in 1973.

Clara Ward was born in Philadelphia in 1924 and was known as the "Charismatic Gospel Queen." A singer, pianist, and composer of over 200 songs, she first sang with the Ward Singers, which included her mother, Gertrude Ward, and her sister, Willa. Gertrude Ward was known for her spirit, and Clara was known for her voice—she loved hymns and the gospel waltz, and also became known for her short phrasing and for her South Carolina moaning. In the 1950s, she toured with Aretha Franklin's father, the Reverend C. L. Franklin of Detroit, and later sang outside the church. She felt that gospel music wasn't meant to be heard only in the church, and she performed at the Apollo Theatre in Harlem, in Las Vegas, at the Newport Jazz Festival, and elsewhere. She died in 1973.

Dinah Washington, originally named Ruth Lee Jones, was born in 1924 in Tuscaloosa, Alabama. As a child, she sang and played piano for her church choir. In 1940, she was hired by Sallie Martin as a piano player, and she later toured with the Roberta Martin Singers. She adopted her stage name in 1943 after she began performing in nightclubs as a rhythm-and-blues singer, where she eventually became known as the "Queen of the Blues." Her trademark was her sound and vocal control. It was because of her passionate style that many early fans remained loyal to Dinah even after she began her solo career in blues and popular music outside the church. She died in 1963.

The Staples Singers were a family gospel group started by Roebuck Staples (bottom in this photograph). Growing up on a Mississippi plantation, he learned to play the guitar, copying the big blues guitarists of the day. In the 1940s, he moved to Chicago and in 1951 set up a family group with his wife, Cleotha, and his children Purvis, Mavis, and Yvonne. They began recording in 1957. During the 1960s and 1970s, they popularized contemporary folk-gospel music.

James Cleveland was born in 1932 and raised in Chicago. He is known as the "Crown Prince of Gospel." As a boy, he sang soprano at the Pilgrim Baptist Church, where the minister of music was Professor Thomas Dorsey. As he grew older, his voice changed dramatically, becoming low and raspy. His idols were members of the Roberta Martin Singers, for whom he eventually played piano and composed songs. In the mid-1950s, he joined a group called the Caravans as an arranger and soon became known for the great feeling he injected into the songs he arranged. He was a modern pioneer in gospel music whose emotional energy was remarkable. He died in 1991.

Shirley Caesar, one of twelve children, was born in 1938 in Durham, North Carolina. Her father, Big Jim Caesar, was a minister and a gospel quartet singer, and at age ten, Shirley was singing with her sisters in churches and schools. By the time she was twelve, her father had passed away, and she began traveling and singing to support her mother. Soon she was known throughout the South as "Baby Shirley." Later she would become a high-energy singer, preacher, and dancer. She traveled with the gospel group the Caravans until 1966. In 1972, she became the first black woman singer to win a Grammy award, and she went on to win several more. She is still singing today and appeared in the tenth anniversary production of *Mama, I Want to Sing* in 1994.

Aretha Franklin was born in 1942 in Memphis. Known as the "Queen of Soul," she was the daughter of the Reverend C. L. Franklin, whose church attracted many well-known singers. James Cleveland, Mahalia Jackson, B. B. King, and Dinah Washington are but a few who paid visits to the home of the Franklin family. Aretha made her first record at the age of twelve, but it wasn't until she was introduced to the Southern soul sound that she found her place in music. She became successful not only as a singer but also as a pianist. She has made more than twenty-two albums, including *Amazing Grace*, a two-album set of gospel songs, which was recorded live in 1972. She continues today to symbolize the essence of what is known as soul.

Whitney Houston was born in 1963 in Newark, New Jersey. Her mother, Cissy Houston, came from a deeply religious family of dedicated church singers. By the age of seventeen, Cissy had formed the New Hope Baptist Church Young Adult Choir, a gospel choir for teenagers. Later, she gathered together cousins and sisters and formed a family group, the Drinkard Singers. She eventually went on to form the Sweet Inspirations, who became the premier female backup group for such great singers as Aretha Franklin. As a young child, Whitney was a regular visitor to the music studios where her mother recorded, and she would also stand in the wings at places like the Apollo Theatre to hear her mom. Despite her mother's success outside the church, gospel singing always remained a strong influence on Whitney, and in 1975, she sang solo for the first time at the New Hope Baptist Church. Soon afterward, she decided she would pursue a singing career like her mother's. Whitney Houston signed her first recording deal and made her album debut in 1985. Now a singer who is known all over the world, she reveals her gospel roots in every song she sings.

For
Further
Reading:

We'll Understand It Better By and By: Pioneering African American Gospel Composers, edited by Bernice Johnson Reagon (Washington, D.C.: Smithsonian Institution, 1992).

The Gospel Sound: Good News and Bad Times, by Anthony Heilbut (New York: Limelight Editions, 1987).

African-American Good News (Gospel) Music, by Sherry Sherrod Du Pree and Herbert C. Du Pree (Washington, D.C.: Middle Atlantic Regional Press, 1993).

A simple, reassuring lullaby, "Jesus Loves Me" is a favorite for and with children. The words were originally part of a popular nineteenth-century American novel, *Say and Seal*, by Anna and Susan Warner. Spoken in the novel to comfort a sick child, the words have endured in the song. William Bradbury, the composer, specialized in children's music. It's quite stirring to hear a two- or three-year-old sing this song as one of the first he or she ever learns in life.

Jesus Loves Me

"We intended gospel to strike a happy medium for the downtrodden. This music lifted people out of the muck and mire of poverty and loneliness, of being broke, and gave them some kind of hope anyway. Make it anything other than good news, it ceases to be gospel."

—Professor Thomas A. Dorsey, the "Father of Gospel"

"Jesus Lifted Me" is a song of deliverance—from captivity, from hardship, from overwhelming problems. It's about being lifted from a sea of sadness, heartache, and pain. The repetition in the song insures that the message and theme come across and become part of the thinking of the listener. Its spirit is jubilant and free.

Jesus Lifted Me

VERSES:

1. *Satan had me bound but Jesus lifted me, (etc.) ~ CHORUS*
2. *When I was in trouble Jesus lifted me, (etc.) ~ CHORUS*

Originally an anonymous Negro spiritual, "He's Got the Whole World in His Hands" was made popular in Southern Baptist church circles in a spirited 1952 choral arrangement by William J. Reynolds. Many popular singers have since included it in their concert performances, broadening its recognition.

A great hand-clapper, toe-tapper, and sing-alonger, this song is usually performed up-tempo, with great energy, joy, and spirit. The repetition of the lyrics gives everyone a chance to participate and feel the joy of singing.

He's Got the Whole World in His Hands

VERSES:

1. He's got the wind and the rain in His hands, (etc.) ~ CHORUS
2. He's got the tiny little baby in His hands, (etc.) ~ CHORUS
3. He's got you and me, brother, [sister] in His hands, (etc.) ~ CHORUS

"Ev'ry Time I Feel de Spirit" is a good example of the nineteenth-century spirituals that built the foundation for twentieth-century gospel music. These spirituals were sung by slaves in the fields, in small country churches, and in one-room schoolhouses, and were passed on by word of mouth. Later, the songs were sung with fuller arrangements and harmonies by church and college choirs—a tribute to the past and an acknowledgment of the power and importance of music in the history of African-American people.

Ev'ry Time I Feel de Spirit

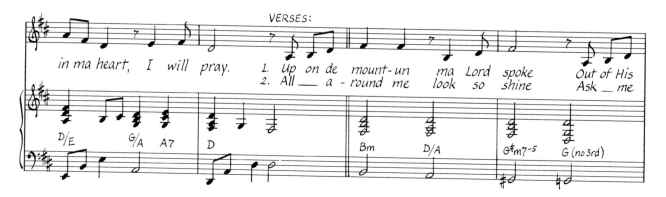

22

mouth came   fire   an'   smoke.   Jor - dan   Riv - er   chilly and
Lord if   all   was   mine.   Ain't but one train   runs   dis

Em9   G/A   A7   G/D   D   Bm   D/A

cold   Chill __ my   bod - y   but not my soul.   Ev - 'ry
track,   It runs to   heav - en   __ an' runs back.   Ev - 'ry

G#m7⁻⁵   G (no 3rd)   Em9   G/A   A7   G/D G/A   D

The words of this song—"It's me, it's me, O Lord"—reflect the New Testament vision of God as available and receptive to every human being on an individual basis. When it is sung and performed with energy, zest, and the desire for direct communication, the singers and audience feel transformed.

It's Me (Standing in the Need of Prayer)

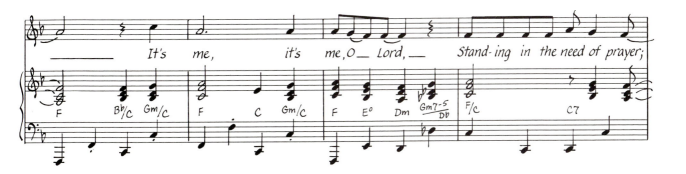

Stand-ing in the need of prayer; ———— Not my sis- ter, not my broth- er, but it's
Stand-ing in the need of prayer; ———— Not my neigh-bor, not a stran-ger, but it's

F   F/C   C7   F   Bb   Am   Gm   F   F/C

CHORUS:

me, O — Lord, ——   Stand-ing in the need of prayer. ———— It's
me, O — Lord, ——   Stand-ing in the need of prayer. ———— It's

F   E°   Dm   Gm7-5/Db   F/C   F/C   C7   F   Bb   Am   Gm

This is a very theatrical piece of music, excellent for choirs giving public performances. While the choir moves in choreographed or spontaneous movement, several soloists can step out to "testify" in each verse. Then these individual singers blend back into the support of the community. The words of the song—"Since I laid my burden down"—are a poetic way of describing the power of gospel music, which encourages the singers to let go of negative emotions, such as fear, worry, anxiety, and anger, and let some positive vibrations come on through!

Glory, Glory, Hallelujah

VERSES:

1. I feel better, so much better (etc.) — CHORUS
2. Burdens down, Lord, burdens down, Lord, (etc.) — CHORUS
3. I'm going home to live with Jesus, (etc.) — CHORUS

In the gospel tradition, clothes and weapons are often metaphors for the attitudes, fears, or worries that can be dissolved through the power of song. For slaves, the words of this song—"I ain't gonna study war no more" and "Gonna put on my long white robe"—proposed a kind of spiritual armor against the trials and hardships of life: rejecting violence or "war" and arming oneself with faith.

Down by the Riverside

stu-dy____ war____ no more._____ I ain't gon-na stu-dy war__ no more,

____ I ain't gon-na stu-dy war__ no more,___ I ain't gon-na stu-dy_____ war no more,

_____ Well, I ain't gon-na stu-dy war__ no more,___ I ain't gon-na stu-dy war__ no more,

____ Ain't gon-na stu-dy_____ war__ no more._____ 2. Gon-na

VERSES:

2. Gonna lay down my sword and shield, (etc.) ~ CHORUS
3. Gonna put on my long white robe, (etc.) ~ CHORUS
4. Gonna meet my loving Savior, (etc.) ~ CHORUS

This is the kind of song that everyone seems to know, no matter where you go: a join-in, feel-good, get-the-hands-clapping, good-for-the-whole-family kind of piece. The words point to the connections between generations and the joy and security of family. Further back, for the slaves transported to the plantations of North America, it helped preserve a connection with their ancestry in Africa.

Old-Time Religion

VERSES:

1. It was good for my dear mother, (etc.) ~ CHORUS
2. It was good for the Hebrew children, (etc.) ~ CHORUS
3. Makes me love everybody, (etc.) ~ CHORUS

This is a song that is recognized and loved the world over, especially in Europe and Japan. The melody is so strong that it invites any soloist to reach down and sing from the heart. It is also a wonderful song for a choir, where power, rhythm, and style can be orchestrated by different vocal parts and harmonies.

As in many gospel songs, the words of "Swing Low, Sweet Chariot" can stand for many things. The "chariot" was a sledlike vehicle used by slaves in the Carolinas to transport tobacco. Later, the "chariot" came to represent a means of escape to freedom in Africa: it was imagined "swinging low" from the skies in order to fly souls away from America and back to the homeland.

Swing Low, Sweet Chariot

"Gospel is the energizing force behind jazz, blues, and popular music. It is the nucleus of African-American music and the connection to the earliest music of the slaves—a free-flowing rhythmic expression of a spirit deep within one's soul. It's good news; it's truth.

"It's my life. It was my beginning, and it will be my end."

—Mavis Staples of the Staples Singers

Whereas some gospel music is strong and solemn, this song is usually performed with a sense of lightness, joy, and bouncy resolution. The melody and rhythm make you want to move, dance, and sing.

I Shall Not Be Moved

VERSES:

1. I'm on my way to heaven, I shall not be moved, (etc.) ~ CHORUS
2. King Jesus is my captain, I shall not be moved, (etc.) ~ CHORUS
3. When my burden's heavy, I shall not be moved, (etc.) ~ CHORUS

This is a very old song, a spiritual that expresses at once the sadness and the strength of a people bound together by injustice. Many slaves found strength in the comparison of their own trials and tribulations working in the fields to the burdens of Jesus—in the words of this song: "Nobody knows the trouble I've seen/Nobody knows but Jesus." Sometimes, when things are going badly, the best thing to do is sing with all your might and soul. Singing lifts the spirit—and this song is definitely an uplifter.

Nobody Knows the Trouble I've Seen

VERSE:

2. Although you see me goin' long so, Oh, yes, Lord!
   I have my troubles here below, Oh, yes, Lord! Oh! ~ CHORUS

"In every gospel song there is a message. In order to deliver it, give it to someone else, you must know the story yourself. That's my policy. Just open up. That's all. That's all I can say. Never had a lesson. I watch a lot of singers. I find it's from here [abdomen] and not from here [throat]. That's my secret."

—Delois Barrett Campbell of the Roberta Martin Singers

"There are songs for different people. Each one of us maybe has a favorite. One song that somebody might sing might not hit you the way this person does it, might not touch you the way it touched this person here. She [Roberta Martin] taught us to present the song as if you were experiencing it yourself."

—Romance Watson of the Roberta Martin Singers

This song is a great example of the call-and-response tradition in gospel music. The leader sings a line and the choir/audience responds quickly so that there is a wonderful give-and-take that builds momentum, energy, and spirit in the entire group.

The words of this spiritual—"I want to be in that number/Oh when the sun refuse to shine"—refer to the biblical Day of Judgment, when believers are reunited with God. It was brought to a popular audience in the early part of the twentieth century by Louis Armstrong. Armstrong's version conjures up the celebratory dancing in the streets of a New Orleans funeral, when people gather to say a rapturous farewell to a departed friend, brother, or sister.

When the Saints Go Marching In

VERSES:
1. Oh when they crown Him Lord of all, (etc.) ~ CHORUS
2. Oh when the sun refuse to shine, (etc.) ~ CHORUS

With its powerful repetition, "Take it to the Lord in prayer," this song likens Jesus to a close personal friend who can lift a burden of grief. The author, Joseph Scriven, whose fiancée drowned the night before they were to be married, later wrote this song to comfort his mother when she was seriously ill. It was one of the most popular hymns in a famous collection called *Stanky's Gospel Hymns: Number One.*

What a Friend

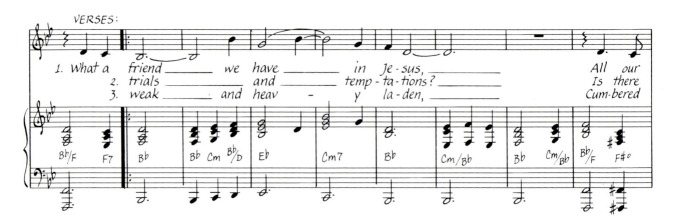

1. What a friend _____ we have _____ in Je-sus, _____ All our
2. trials _____ and _____ temp - ta - tions? _____ Is there
3. weak _____ and heav - y la - den, _____ Cum-bered

sins ____ and griefs ____ to bear! _____ What a
trou - ble an - y - where? _____ We should
with ____ a load ____ of care? _____ Pre-cious

pri - vi - lege ____ to car - ry ____ Ev - ery-
nev - er be ____ dis - cour - aged, ____ Take it
Sav - ior, still ____ our ref - uge, ____ Take it

thing ____ to God ____ in pray'r! _____ O ___ what
to ____ the Lord ____ in pray'r. _____ Can ___ we
to ____ the Lord ____ in pray'r. _____ Do ___ thy

peace ____ we of - ten for-feit, _____ O ___ what
find ____ a friend ____ so faith-ful _____ who ___ will
friends ____ des - pise, ____ for - sake thee? _____ Take ___ it

45

"Gospel is the message of Jesus Christ.

"It is the music of the heart.

"It teaches us how to live.

"God is my all and all, he is everything to me."

—Deniece Williams, singer, songwriter, and producer

Thomas Ken was a bold, rebellious chaplain in the Church of England who spoke out so forcefully against corruption in both the religious and political establishments of his time that he was imprisoned by King James II. He fought for the right to express the power and glory of God in all ways, whether or not prescribed by the Church, and wanted his students to sing as a means of praise. In modern gospel music, singing is very much a means of praise. This doxology, sung with dignity and a sense of personal connection to the presence of God within, unlocks deep emotion.

Doxology (Praise God)

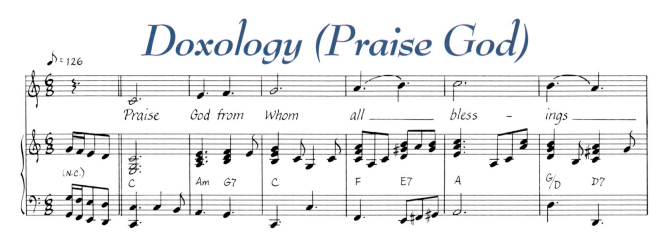

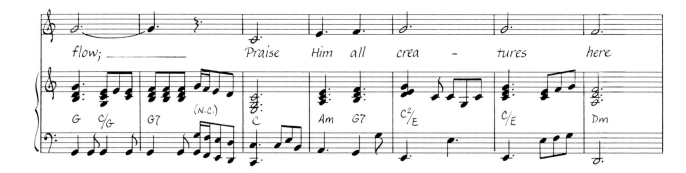

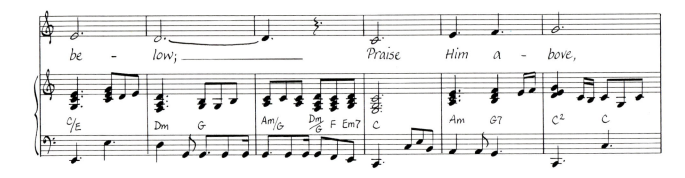

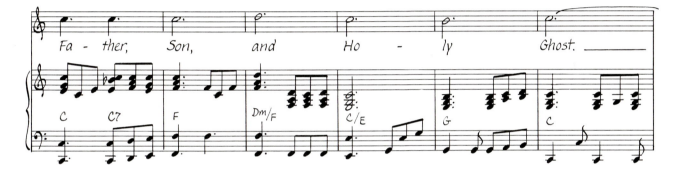

This is what is sometimes called a "triumphing" song: it expresses a feeling of being on top of the world. A bright, bouncy song, it's one to sing along with—especially when riding in a car or on a bus trip, when singers start to improvise different harmonies and parts of the basic melody.

Do, Lord, Remember Me

VERSES:

1. I've got a home in the glory land, that outshines the sun, (x3)
   'Way beyond the sun. ~ CHORUS
2. I took Jesus as my Savior, you take Him too, (x3)
   'Way beyond the blue. ~ CHORUS

This stirring composition captures the spirit of the gospel movement—and was one of the earliest gospel hits written by a woman. Fanny Crosby, who wrote the words, was blind, yet she wrote more than 8,000 gospel song texts. Her partner, Phoebe Knapp, wrote more than 500 gospel songs, including the music for this one.

We have auditioned thousands of people for the gospel musical *Mama, I Want to Sing,* and more people, both men and women, have chosen this as their audition song than any other musical composition. This song can show the range and the power of a singer. If you can sing this piece with power, grace, and emotional impact, you've got the gift of song. It is an excellent performance piece for the solo singer!

Blessed Assurance

va - tion, pur - chase of God, Born of His Spir - it, washed in His
wait - ing, look - ing a - bove, Filled with His good - ness, lost in His

C G/D C/E F C Dm/F F/G G7

CHORUS:

blood. This is my sto - ry, this is my song, Prais - ing my
love.

Csus4 Gsus4 C F C

Sav - ior all the day long. This is my sto - ry, this is my

Am D7 G Dm/G C C/E F

VERSE:

song, Prais - ing my Sav - ior all the day long. 2. Per - fect sub -

C C/E Dm/F F6/G G7 C FMA7 Dm/G F/G

"Amazing Grace" combines a beautiful, simple melody with a lyric that affirms the power of faith in action. When sung full out, from the heart and gut, this song releases a tremendous emotional power. One of the most popular of all gospel songs, it actually has a dark shadow over it: it was written by the captain of a slave ship. John Newton was transporting slaves to the Americas when, in March 1748, he survived a particularly violent storm at sea. The experience led to a religious conversion, and at age thirty-nine Newton was ordained as a minister by the Anglican church.

The melody comes from an early American folk tune known as "Loving Lambs."

Amazing Grace

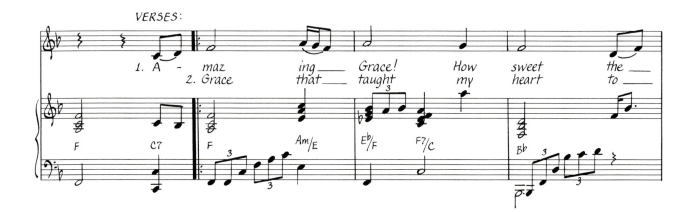

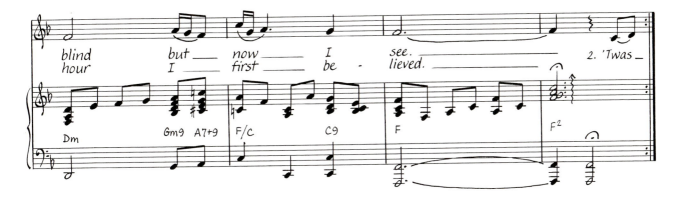

"Gospel is the love and joy of my life.

"Gospel music is a type of music that brings joy where there is sorrow, brings peace where there is confusion. It is hope where there is none, brings sunshine where there is rain, and makes victors out of victims.

"When the anointing comes for a person who is singing it, everything about them changes."

—Pastor Shirley Caesar, seven-time Grammy award winner

The words of this song point out that the strength of any "house"—or faith—depends on the strength of its foundation. Writer Edward Mote, the son of poor London innkeepers, became a minister, as well as the author of more than 150 hymns. "Solid Rock" is a wonderful choral number, generating much power, harmony, and rhythm. In *Mama, I Want to Sing*, it has been performed as the opening scene of the show to get the audience rocking.

Solid Rock

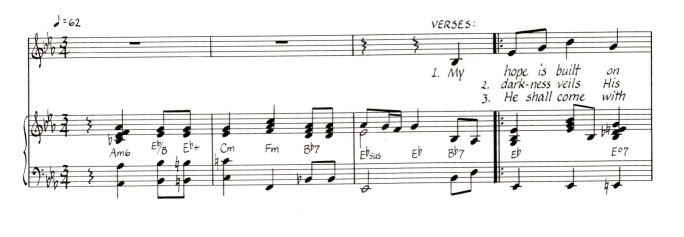

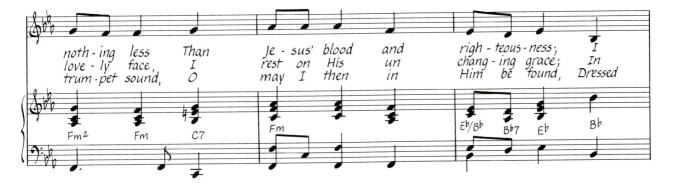

dare not trust the sweet-est frame, But whol-ly lean on
ev-ery high and storm-y gale My an-chor holds within His righ-teous - ness a - lone, Fault - less to stand be

E♭ E°7 Fm2 Fm C7/G Fm Fm/B♭

CHORUS:

Je - sus' name.
in the veil. } On Christ, the sol - id rock, I stand; All
fore the throne.

E♭/B♭ B♭7 E♭ E♭ B♭7/F E♭/G Fm/A♭ E♭/G Fm

VERSES:

oth - er ground is sink - ing sand, All oth - er ground is sink - ing sand. 2)
3) when

E♭/B♭ E♭ F9 B♭7 E♭ A♭MA7/E♭ B♭7 E♭ B♭

This song is most meaningful to me. Once, when I was in the hospital for surgery, going "under" from the anesthesia but never quite losing total consciousness, I heard this song, buried deep in my soul, being sung by the choir of my church, where my father was the pastor. He had died when I was only one year old, but I saw him standing in the pulpit singing this song with the choir. I knew I was going to be all right!

Horatio Spafford wrote the words to "It Is Well with My Soul" as a way to cope with grief when his four daughters were drowned in a shipping accident in November 1873. Composer Philip Bliss wrote several hundred religious songs in his short lifetime.

It Is Well with My Soul

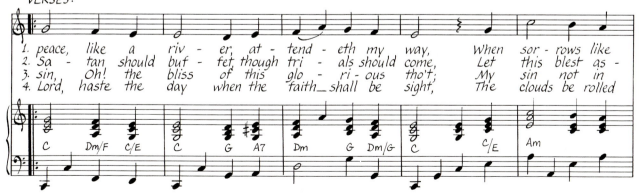

sea bil - lows roll. _____ What - ev - er my lot, Thou hast
sur - ance con - trol, _____ That Christ has re - gard - ed my
part, but the whole, _____ Is nailed to the cross and I
back as a scroll, _____ The trump shall re - sound and the

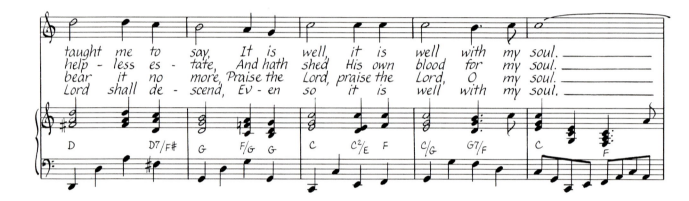

taught me to say, It is well, it is well with my soul. _____
help - less es - tate, And hath shed His own blood for my soul. _____
bear it no more, Praise the Lord, praise the Lord, O my soul. _____
Lord shall de - scend, Ev - en so it is well with my soul. _____

CHORUS:

It is well, _____ with my soul, _____ It __ is __

well, it is well with my soul. _____ 2. Though
3. My
4. And,

Participation and energy are fundamental parts of the gospel experience. You don't just sit there on the sidelines: when you start to sing, you are right there in the middle of the action, and singing gospel becomes an emotional and spiritual release that fortifies you for the other games of life. "Just a Little Talk with Jesus" is another gospel favorite that moves right along, making your hands want to clap, your foot want to tap, and your heart want to zap everything that's going wrong in the world around you.

Just a Little Talk with Jesus

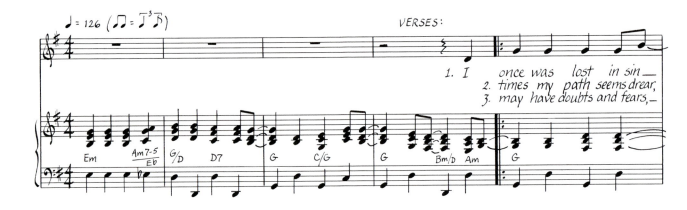

heav-en filled my soul; _____ It bathed my heart in love ____ and
hide the light of day; _____ The mists of sin may rise ____ and
watch-es day and night; _____ I go with Him in pray'r, ____ He

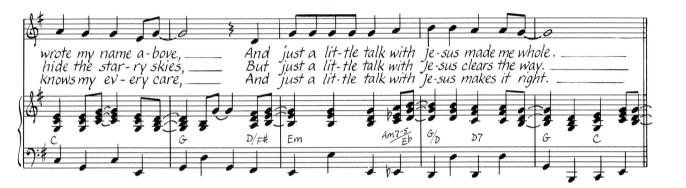

wrote my name a-bove, ____ And just a lit-tle talk with Je-sus made me whole. ____
hide the star-ry skies, ____ But just a lit-tle talk with Je-sus clears the way.
knows my ev-ery care, ____ And just a lit-tle talk with Je-sus makes it right. ____

CHORUS:

Now let us have a lit-tle talk with Je - sus; We will tell Him all a-bout our

trou-bles, He will hear our faint-est cry, ____ He will ans-wer by and by. ____

"The fight for rights here in Memphis was pretty rough on the black church. . . . Before the freedom fights started, before Martin Luther King days, I had to lead a lot of protest meetings. In order to get my message over, there were things that were almost dangerous to say—but you could sing it."

—Reverend William Herbert Brewster, pioneering gospel composer

This song was composed by Charles Albert Tindley—a colorful and dynamic minister who served in Philadelphia in the early 1900s. Tindley was a great preacher, a publisher of both sermons and songs, and an important influence on the gospel tradition. His songs were recorded by the famous Pace Jubilee Singers and were popular with singers such as Rosetta Tharpe and Marion Williams. This one, often sung at funerals, speaks of enduring difficult situations in life and of how they can be appreciated as turning points.

We'll Understand It Better By and By

that God will lead___ us to that bless-ed prom-ised land;___ But He'll guide
dered in the dark-ness, hea-vy-heart-ed and a-lone;___ But we're trust-

F   G7   Gm7   Bb/C

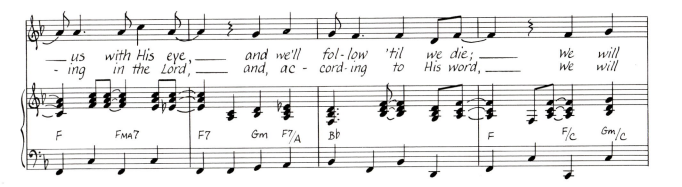

___us with His eye,___ and we'll fol-low 'til we die;___ We will
-ing in the Lord,___ and, ac-cord-ing to His word,___ We will

F   FMA7   F7   Gm   F7/A   Bb   F   F/C   Gm/C

CHORUS:

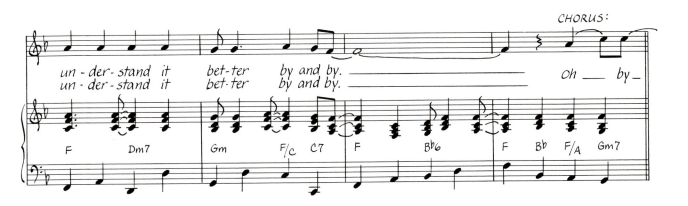

un-der-stand it bet-ter by and by.___
un-der-stand it bet-ter by and by.___ Oh___ by___

F   Dm7   Gm   F/C   C7   F   Bb6   F   Bb   F/A   Gm7

___ and by,___ when the morn-ing comes,___ When___

F   Gm/C   F   Gm/C   F   F7   Bb   F   Am/C   Gm/C

all the saints_ of__ God come gath-er-ing home, __ We will

tell the sto - ry how we've o - ver-come; __ We will

un - der - stand it bet-ter by and by. _____ 2. Oft our cher-

"During the Depression years, many sought solace in church attendance. There was little or no money in the church coffers. The nation was continually being told that prosperity was just around the corner. Many ministers or employees either did not receive salaries or payments were in arrears. A mood of depression prevailed. Suddenly on the horizon appeared gospel music. The word *gospel* means 'good news.'"

—Leona Price of the Roberta Martin Singers

Not all gospel favorites come out of stress or turmoil. Annie Hawks led a safe, secure—even serene—life. One day in 1872, as she was home alone doing simple household chores, she was filled with an overpowering sense of gratitude for the many blessings of her life. She spontaneously wrote down the words of this song. Later she showed them to her pastor, the Reverend Robert Lowry, who wrote the music to accompany them. The song was first performed publicly at the National Baptist Sunday School Convention in Cincinnati in 1872.

I Need Thee Every Hour

cious _____ Lord; No ten - der voice like

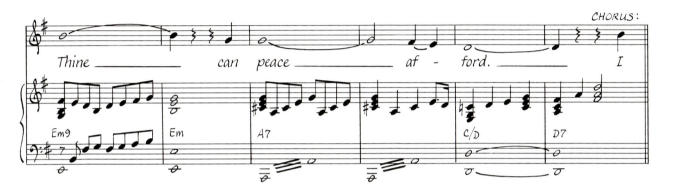

CHORUS:

Thine _____ can peace _____ af - ford. _____ I

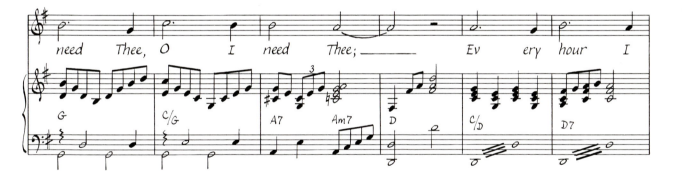

need Thee, O I need Thee; _____ Ev - ery hour I

need Thee! _____ O bless me now, my Sav -

ior,   I   come   to _____ Thee! _____   2. I

VERSES:

2. I need Thee every hour, Stay Thou nearby; Temptations lose their power when Thou art nigh. ~ CHORUS
3. I need Thee every hour, In joy or pain; Come quickly and abide, Or life is vain. ~ CHORUS
4. I need Thee every hour, Most Holy One; O make me Thine indeed, Thou blessed Son! ~ CHORUS

"Gospel is, at bottom, a collective expression of a community long oppressed by injustice that reveals indomitable faith. It is marked by enthusiastic performance, pronounced rhythms. Deeply biblical and testimonial in character, it is the urban spiritual of our day. It is an art form that in the last decade has become universally acclaimed, worldwide."

—Wyatt Tee Walker, author and cultural historian

"Gospel music expresses a unique world view—one that intertwines the spiritual dimension of African-American life with the cultural and the historical.

"It is a testimony about the powers of Jesus Christ and his teachings of spiritual deliverance, inner strength, and racial and social equality.

"Gospel music is simply an expression of African-American religious and cultural sensibilities."

—Dr. Portia K. Maultsby,
ethnomusicologist and professor of Afro-American Studies,
Indiana University

"Deep River" originated in Guilford County, North Carolina, where Quakers bought slaves with the intention of returning them to Africa. One Negro Quaker sea captain, Paul Cuffee, made several trips to Africa in the early nineteenth century, carrying many slaves to their original homes. Along with such small successes, the words of this song—"Deep river, Lord, I want to cross over into camp ground"—encouraged the deep desire of slaves to return to the motherland and reestablish their pride, self-esteem, identity, and independence.

Deep River

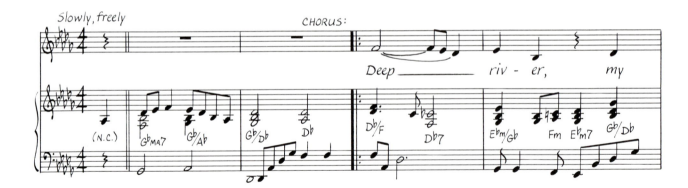

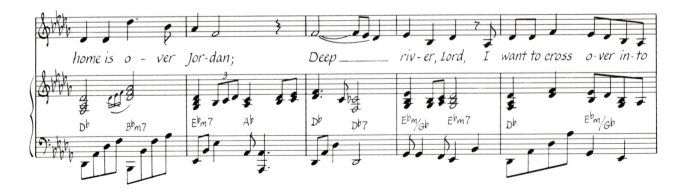

Many hymns were "written" spontaneously in the context of a church service or a Sunday school teaching session. The simple words of this song are obviously for and about children. It appeared in children's songbooks in the 1880s and 1890s and was made popular in a collection called *Child Songs*, edited by Carey Bonner, who gave it a new arrangement. Like many of the most moving gospel songs, it was written by an unknown author and found new life years later.

Praise Him, All Ye Little Children

VERSES:

2. Love Him, love Him, all ye little children, (etc.)
3. Thank Him, thank Him, all ye little children, (etc.)

This song has a wonderful rhythm and build to it. Power is generated through the repetition of the words and the simplicity of the melody—especially when it is sung by many voices. This kind of basic melody invites an imaginative musical director to play with rhythms, harmonies, and modulations so that by the end of the song—perhaps with a few smashing solo riffs in between—a powerful, thrilling climax can be reached that gets a whole congregation or audience to participate and sing along.

Hush! Hush!

Hush! hush! some-bo-dy's call-in' my___ name; Oh, my Lord,___

___ Oh, my Lord, ___ what shall I do? _____

VERSES:

1. *Sounds like Jesus, somebody's callin' my name; (etc.)* ~ CHORUS
2. *Soon one morning, Death's comin' in my room; (etc.)* ~ CHORUS
3. *Run, sinner, run, find yo a hidin' place; (etc.)* ~ CHORUS

"When I was a teenager playing the piano in my local church, there was always a difference between what the notes on the paper read and what I played. For example, the hymnal in front of me notated 'Amazing Grace'—but the gospel sound had an authenticity and originality that was not in the hymnal. I always wanted to preserve what actually happened in church on Sunday morning, almost like writing down stories from an oral tradition."

—Wesley Naylor, musical director of *Mama, I Want to Sing*

So much of both the early spirituals and later twentieth-century gospel music is about what the singer puts in. Simple songs like this, with lyrics that read and play like affirmations, allow a power and rhythm to build. In the words of this song, there is an uplifting vision of salvation, redemption, and love—made all the more powerful by the energy and flow of the music.

God Is Good

VERSES:

2. Jesus is real, Jesus is real. Jesus is real, He's so real to me.
3. He saved my soul, He saved my soul. He saved my soul, and He made me whole.
4. I praise His name, I praise His name. I praise His name, He's so good to me.

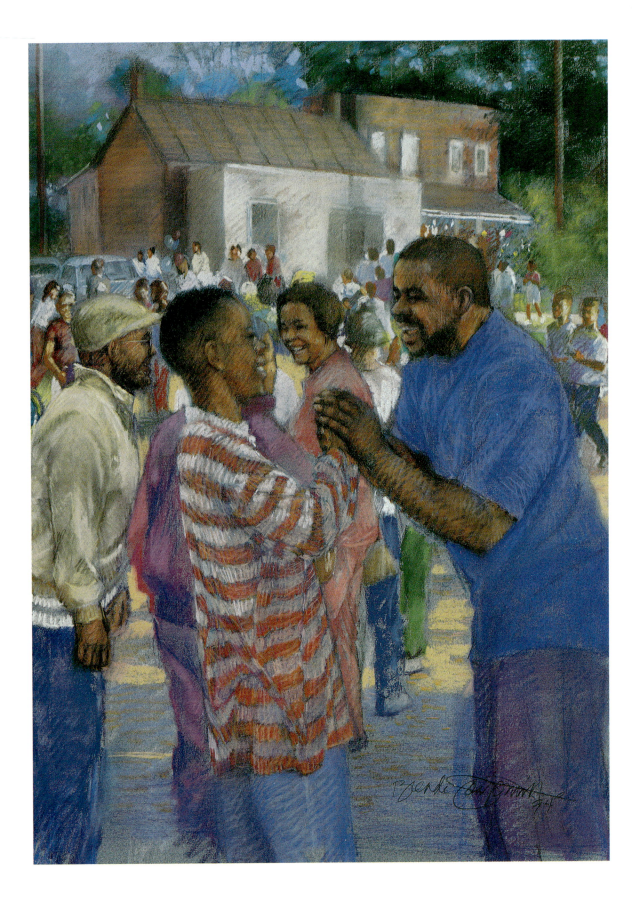

The text of this song was written by Frederick Whitfield and appeared in his collection *Sacred Poems and Prose*. The tune is of unknown origin, but the simple, lilting style is typical of the outdoor camp meetings, where people gathered in natural settings to worship. As is true with so many gospel songs, the power of the melody lies in the arrangement and choral harmonies.

Oh, How I Love Jesus

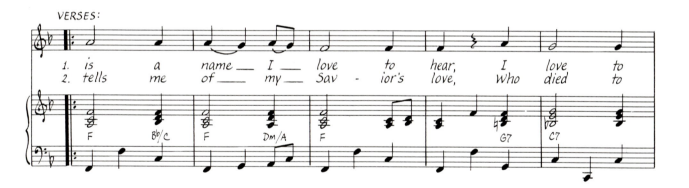

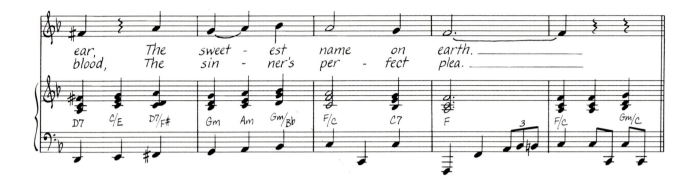

ear, The sweet - est name on earth. _____
blood, The sin - ner's per - fect plea. _____

D7　C/E　D7/F#　Gm　Am　Gm/Bb　F/C　C7　F　F/C　Gm/C

CHORUS:

Oh, How I love Je - sus, Oh, How I love

F　F/C　Bb/C　F/C　Gm/F　F　G7　C7　Bb/D　E°　Bb/D　C7

Je - sus, _____ Oh, How I love Je

F/C　Gm/Bb　F/C　Gm/C　F　A7　Dm　A7

VERSE:

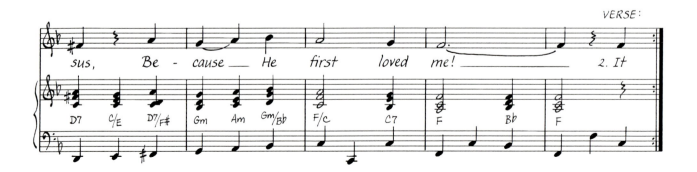

sus, Be - cause ____ He first loved me! _____ 2. It

D7　C/E　D7/F#　Gm　Am　Gm/Bb　F/C　C7　F　Bb　F

This is a song that is recognized all around the globe. It is the song we sing after the curtain call in *Mama, I Want to Sing*, and it is heartwarming to hear Japanese, German, Italian, Turkish, and many other voices joining in, singing with the cast. The words of the song clearly have many levels of meaning. Light can mean "talent," "vision," "hope," "energy," "love"—or anything else that the singer wants to fill in. The repetition, both in the verse and the chorus, is rooted in the spirituals of the nineteenth century. As the words are repeated over and over again, with slight variations, much power is generated.

This Little Light of Mine

VERSES:

1. Everywhere I go, I'm gonna let it shine! (etc.) ~ CHORUS
2. All in my heart, I'm gonna let it shine! (etc.) ~ CHORUS
3. All in my room, I'm gonna let it shine! (etc.) ~ CHORUS

Like so many African-American spirituals with unknown authors, "I'm So Glad" has a symbolic dimension beyond the literal meaning of the words. Looking out on a world of "trouble"—hard work, beatings, lynchings, and seeing family sold on the auction block like cattle—the composer of the spiritual would turn within, to the mind and spirit. Words such as "my heart," "a biding place," even "religion" point to a sense of an inner world, and singing them relieved some of the day-to-day pressure of slavery.

I'm So Glad

I'm so glad trou-ble don't last al - ways,

I'm so glad trou-ble don't last al - ways, ___ Oh, my Lord,

___ Oh, my Lord, ___ what shall I do? ___

VERSES:

1. I'm so glad my soul's got a biding place, (etc.) ~ CHORUS
2. I'm so glad I've got my religion in time, (etc.) ~ CHORUS
3. I'm so glad the devil can do me no harm, (etc.) ~ CHORUS

This song was written by "Miss Lucie" Campbell in 1919 and dedicated to a blind singer named Connie Rosemond, who played his guitar on Beale Street in Memphis, Tennessee. One day, Connie was playing hymns and spirituals, his feet wrapped up against the cold, rainy winter weather with used burlap rags. Some local men, fresh out of a bar, asked him to play some "good ole Southern blues," offering to tip him five dollars. Connie refused, saying he could play only songs that came from "something within." Miss Lucie, who was shopping at a fish market, witnessed the scene and was moved to write this hymn. It brought her national recognition—and, at the National Baptist Convention in 1919, it was performed by the blind street singer Connie Rosemond himself.

Something Within

sol - diers on great bat-tle - fields;   When to their
in me, that ban - ish-es pain;   Some-thing with -
some - thing, that nev - er doth tire?   Oh, if you

Am7   D7   C/D   G   Am/G   G

plead - ings my poor heart did yield,   All I could
in me, I can - not ex - plain,   All that I
have it, that heav - en - ly Fire,   Let the world

Dm7   G²   G   CMA7   Am7   Bm/A   Am

say,   There is some-thing with - in.   (CHOR:) Some-thing with -
know,   There is some-thing with - in.   2. Have you that
know,   There is some-thing with - in.   (CHOR:) Some-thing with -

G/B   Em   G+/D#   G/D   Am   D7   G   C/G   G   G   F#   G

"Gospel is singing about the good news of God!

"Gospel feels like fire shut up in your bones.

"Gospel means Christ lives."

—Reverend Calvin O. Butts III,
pastor of the Abyssinian Baptist Church,
New York City

Index
of
First
Lines